SHAKESPEARE IN THE PUBLIC RECORDS

Frontispiece: Engraving of William Shakespeare by Martin Droeshout from the first folio edition of the plays, 1623.

PUBLIC RECORD OFFICE

Shakespeare

IN THE PUBLIC RECORDS

Text and selection of documents by David Thomas

Section on the will and signatures by Jane Cox
Photographs by John Millen

LONDON   HER MAJESTY'S STATIONERY OFFICE

© *Crown copyright 1985*
First published 1985

ISBN 0 11 440192 6

Design by HMSO: Ian Dobson
Cover illustration: Roy Knipe

CONTENTS

Preface

The life of William Shakespeare has fascinated scholars and others for nearly four hundred years; vast libraries have been assembled and the town of Stratford-upon-Avon preserved as a shrine. Because none of Shakespeare's personal papers survive - there are no letters, notes or drafts - speculation has been rife as to the 'true' authorship of his plays. Biographers and literary critics have argued that such extraordinary genius could not have flowered in an ill-educated family of farming stock. It is worth remembering that among the tangle of fancies and forgeries there is a clear thread of facts about a man called William Shakespeare who spent part of his life in Stratford and part in the theatrical world of London.

Shakespeare's biographers have used various sorts of source material, starting with the stories of him told by contemporaries. Later scholars, not content with repeating the previous generation's version of events, sought confirmation of rumours from the archives kept by church and government. His baptism and burial were identified in the Stratford parish registers and references to his marriage were found in the diocesan records. The muniments of Stratford town council, manor court rolls and registers kept by the local church court were searched and evidence was found.[1] This book is concerned with the documentation of Shakespeare and his family which is now in the Public Record Office in London: the evidence found in the records of central government and the law courts. He appears as a taxpayer, a property owner, a will maker, a beneficiary in the wills of others, an actor under royal patronage, a shareholder in theatres, a dramatist and is involved in law suits. This information has been brought to light gradually by the industry and application of researchers who, over the years, have worked systematically through the most inaccessible and obscure material. Chance discoveries have been made and are still being made. Listed here are all the known Shakespeare documents in the Public Record Office; the major items are reproduced and described, including two references to Shakespeare's father which were discovered in April 1983.[2]

[1]The fullest documentation of Shakespeare's life is given in S. Schoenbaum, *William Shakespeare, A Documentary Life* (London, 1975).

[2]See documents 3 and 4.

1. Stratford Court Leet, 29 April 1552 (SC 2/207/82). Translation: Item [the jurors] present on their oaths that Humphrey Reynoldes (XII d.), Adrian Quyney (XII d.) and John Shakyspere (XII d.) made a refuse heap in a street called Hendley Street against the order of the court.

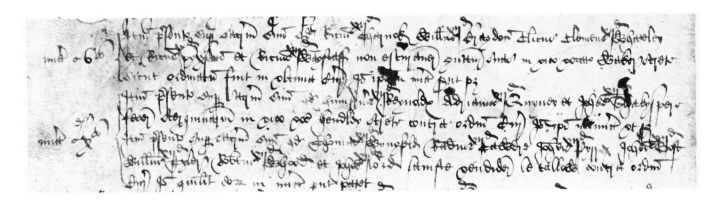

The Birthplace, two houses converted into one in Henley Street, Stratford, which are probably those mentioned in the 1590 survey.

I Shakespeare's Father

John Shakespeare, William's father, was a glove maker and wool dealer. He left the farm at Snitterfield near Stratford where he was born and served his apprenticeship in Stratford. His first appearance in the public records, twelve years before his son's birth, is far from a dramatic entry; he was fined a shilling by the local court for making a rubbish dump in Henley Street. There was an authorized dump at the other end of the road.

This incident suggests that John Shakespeare was living in Henley Street in 1552. In 1556 he acquired from one Edward West a house and garden in Henley Street for which he paid a rent of sixpence a year to the lord of the manor, the Earl of Warwick. A survey made in 1590 (document 2), when the earl died and the property fell to the crown, shows that John had the sixpenny house and another larger property in Henley Street which he rented for thirteen pence a year. This second house may have been where he was living at the time of the rubbish dump prosecution. Some time in the late sixteenth century two adjoining houses in the street were converted into one large house, the building now known as the Birthplace, where tradition has it that Mary Arden gave birth to William Shakespeare and her seven other children.

2. Survey of 1590 (E 178/2351), showing John Shakespeare holding two tenements with appurtenances in Henley Street, one rented at sixpence a year, the other at thirteen pence.

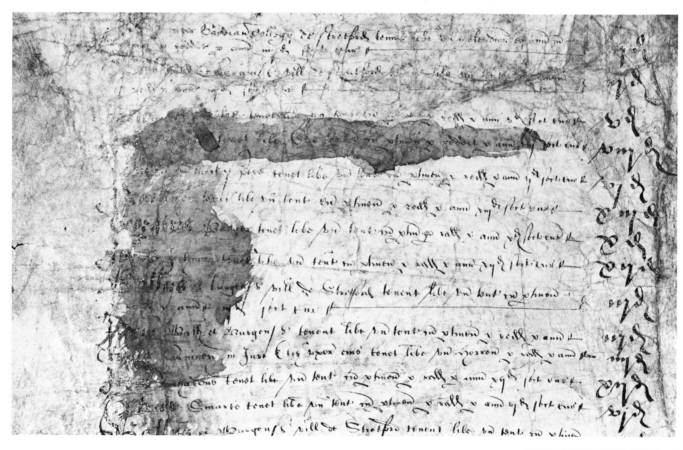

John Shakespeare had an extremely successful career until William was eight or nine. He was active in the town's adminstration, rising through the ranks of aletaster, constable, principal burgess and chamberlain. In 1565 he became an alderman and in 1567 he achieved the chief borough office of bailiff. Some recently discovered actions in the Court of Exchequer give some idea of the scale of his business activities, endorsing the story passed on by the Restoration actor Thomas Betterton that he was 'a considerable dealer in wool'. In 1570 John was twice accused of breaking the stringent usury laws by making loans of £80 and £100 to Walter Musshem or Mussum[1] of Walton D'Eiville, a village not far from Stratford and charging £20 interest in both cases. Musshem appears to have been a business partner of John Shakespeare; in 1573 they were jointly sued for debt by one Henry Higford.[2]

[1] Musshem has not been positively identified but he was probably a sheep farmer who died in 1588 and whose probate inventory is in the Worcester County Record Office. This Musshem was possessed of a personal estate worth £114 8s. 4d., including 117 sheep, at his death.

[2] CP 40/1313 m.399; 1355 m.7d; 1356 m.1123d.

3. *Exchequer Memoranda Roll, Hilary 1570 (E 159/359, Recorda, Hil. m.237), John 'Shappere alias Shakespere' of 'Stratford upon Haven' accused of lending money at interest to John Musshem.*

Two years later John Shakespeare faced accusations of illegal wool-dealing. A statute of 1552, designed to protect the merchants of the Staple, forbade the purchase of wool by private individuals. It was claimed that John Shakespeare had purchased 200 tods (i.e. 5,600 pounds) of wool in Westminster and a further 100 tods at Snitterfield; both offences took place in 1571. His total expenditure on wool was £210.

For one of the usury offences he was fined forty shillings and the other cases ended inconclusively. He probably escaped official punishment by coming to a private arrangement with the professional informer who is known to have brought three of the cases to court, the notorious James Langrake. This unsavoury character had been accused of raping one of his servants, had been imprisoned for accepting money from the people he informed against and was later fined and banned for a year from bringing further informations.

4. Exchequer Memoranda Roll, Michaelmas 1572 (E 159/363, Recorda, Mich. m.183d), John Shakespeare accused of illegal wool dealing.

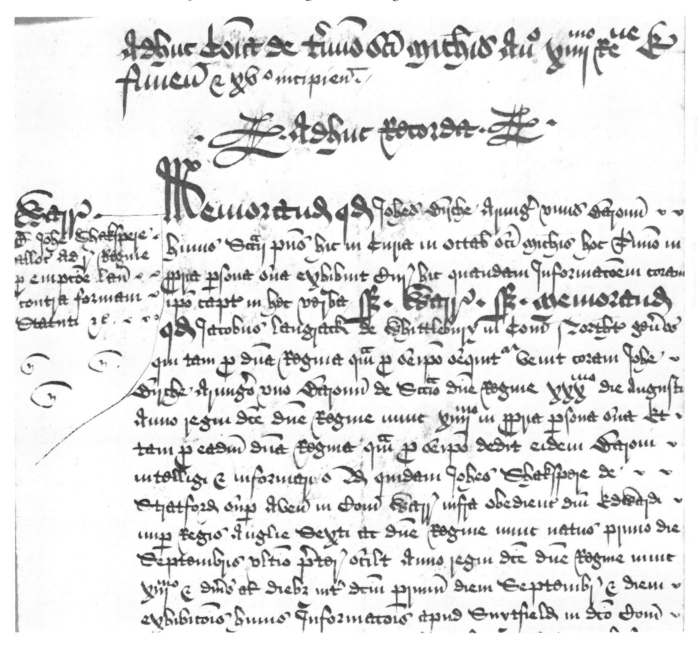

5. Second certificate of the Privy Council commissioners for Warwickshire concerning recusants, 25 September 1592 (SP 12/243/76), John Shakespeare is shown as not going to church for fear of process for debt.

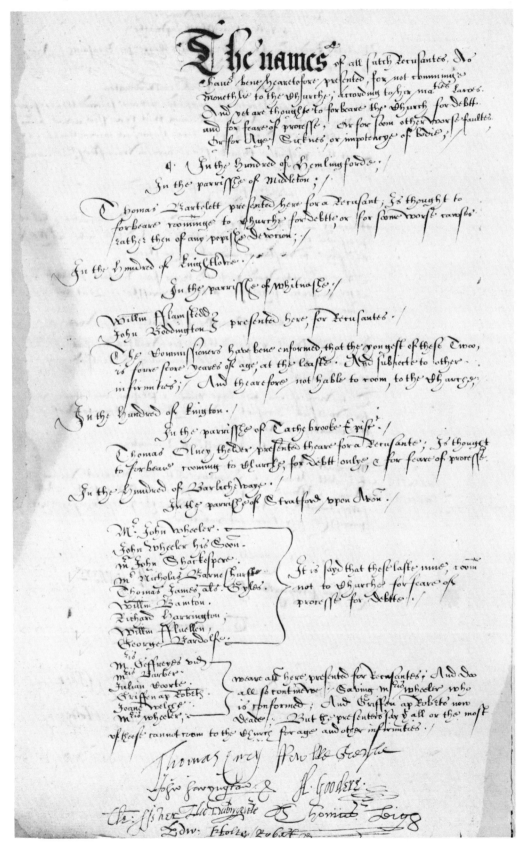

For reasons yet to be discovered, John Shakespeare withdrew from public life in Stratford: in 1576 he stopped attending council meetings and in 1586 he was replaced as alderman. His business evidently suffered and by 1591 he was avoiding his creditors. In this year Privy Council commissioners were appointed in each county to hunt out Jesuits and seminary priests and identify those people (known as recusants) who failed to attend church. The second report of the Warwickshire commissioners has survived. It lists prosecuted recusants, those who had left the county, those who had conformed and those who 'forbeare the Church for debtt and for feare of processe, Or for soom other worse faultes. Or for Age, Sicknes or impotencye of bodie'. Among the names of those who were afraid to appear in public in case they were prosecuted for debt is that of Shakespeare's father. Also hiding from the law, or from their creditors, were William Fluellen and George Bardolfe. Did Shakespeare remember these old associates of his father when he was writing Henry V?

It was his father's need to borrow money which was the occasion of the first reference to William Shakespeare in the public records. In 1578 John borrowed £40 from Edmund Lambert on the security of a property in Wilmcote in the parish of Aston Cantlow. The condition of the transaction was that John Shakespeare would repay the money in 1580. The Shakespeares had acquired the property in 1556 when Robert Arden had bequeathed to his daughter Mary (Shakespeare's mother) 'all my land in Willmcote cawlide Asbyes and the crop apone the grounde sowne and tyllide as hitt is'. The exact site of Asbies is not known. John Shakespeare did not repay the £40, instead he brought an action in the court of King's Bench against Edmund Lambert's son, John, in 1589, claiming that Lambert senior (now presumably dead) had agreed to buy the land outright for £20. John and Mary Shakespeare and their heir, William, had agreed to this, but the money had never been paid. A date was set for a formal hearing, but after the initial entry of the pleading on the plea roll there is no more record of the case. Evidently the damages claimed by the Shakespeares were never paid because eight years later John Shakespeare tried to recover Asbies in the court of Chancery. This time he said that he had offered to repay the £40 to Lambert but the latter had refused either to accept the money or return the property until Shakespeare had paid off other debts owing to him. Once again there is no record of this matter being settled.

6. The complaint of John Shakespeare in the court of King's Bench against John Lambert, son of Edmund Lambert, late of Barton-on-the-Heath, Warwickshire, 1589 (KB 27/1311 rot.516), the earliest reference to William Shakespeare in the public records.

II Shakespeare in London

While his father's fortunes were in decline William Shakespeare, now in his mid or late twenties, moved from Stratford to London. At eighteen he had married Ann Hathaway, a local farmer's daughter, much older than himself; three children were born, Susanna in May 1583, six months after the marriage, and twins, Judith and Hamnet, two years later. Some time between 1585 and 1593 Shakespeare left his young family to pursue his career as actor and writer.

Among the public records there is considerable documentation of his life in London. In 1596 he was bound over to keep the peace; for the years 1597-1600 there are tax certificates; in 1604 he was involved in a law suit. References to his professional life and the activities of his company are to be found spanning the years 1595 to 1611.

The earliest non-theatrical reference discovered 54 years ago by Leslie Hotson, is dated 1596. By this time Shakespeare was a member of the Lord Chamberlain's company and had written at least seven plays. In the spring there was a violent quarrel between William Gardiner, a Bankside justice of the peace, and his step-son, William Wayte. Later in the year Francis Langley, builder and owner of the new Swan theatre in Southwark, became involved and some time in the Michaelmas term, Wayte sought sureties of the peace from the court of King's Bench against Langley, Dorothy Soer, wife of John Soer, Ann Lee and William Shakespeare 'for fear of death'. Such a procedure was commonplace; the usual practice was that King's Bench issued a writ of attachment to the sheriff of the county concerned, who then arrested the troublemakers and brought them to court where they gave bonds to keep the peace. Nothing has yet come to light to explain what the quarrel was about or to clarify Shakespeare's part in it. The two women named in the writ have not been identified.

7. King's Bench entry of writ of attachment, Michaelmas, 1596 (KB 29/234). Translation: Be it known that William Wayte seeks sureties of the peace against William Shakspere, Francis Langley, Dorothy Soer, wife of John Soer, and Ann Lee for fear of death and so forth [Writ of] attachment to the sherriff of Surrey.

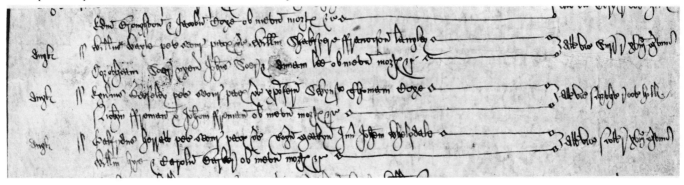

There are five documents which relate to Shakespeare as a taxpayer. In 1593 Parliament granted the crown three subsidies or taxes on goods. The last of these three taxes was to be paid in two instalments, one in 1595-6 at the rate of 1s. 8d. in the pound and the other in February 1597 at the rate of 1s. in the pound. A certificate submitted by the London tax commissioners and dated 15 November 1597 (document 8) shows that Shakespeare's goods were valued at £5 and that he therefore owed 5s. for the second instalment of the subsidy.

8. Certificate of the London tax commissioners showing Shakespeare in St Helen's Bishopsgate as a defaulter on a tax payment of 5s. 15 November 1597 (E 179/146/354).

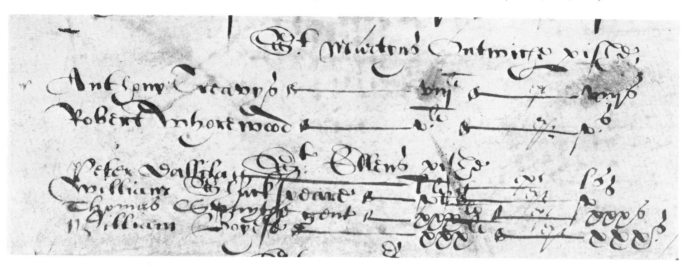

9. Indenture by the London tax commissioners listing Shakespeare among the tax defaulters in St Helen's Bishopsgate, 1 October 1598. His goods are valued at £5 (E 179/146/369).

He was assessed as a resident of the parish of St Helen's Bishopsgate, but is noted as being among those who 'are all ether dead dep|ar|t|ed| and gone out of the sayde warde or their goodes soe eloigned or conveyed out of the same or in such pryvate or Coverte manner kepte whereby the severall somes ... on them ... assessed ... nether might nor could ... be leveyed of them'.

Three more subsidies were granted to the crown in 1597, the first of which was payable by 1 October 1598. Shakespeare again appears as a Bishopsgate resident owning personal property to the value of £5, this time in a tax commissioners' indenture (document 9). Against his name is the word 'affid|avit|', indicating that he had not paid the 13*s.* 4*d.* tax which he owed the Exchequer. In the main account, known as the Pipe Roll (document 10) for 1598-9 and 1599-1600 his debt of 13*s.* 4*d.* is noted. The entry on the second roll is particularly interesting. The debt of 13*s.* 4*d.* is listed as the business of the sheriff of Surrey and Sussex and was referred, according to the marginal note, to the bishop of Winchester ('Ep|iscop|o Winton|ensi|'). The only area in either county where the bishop had jurisdiction was the liberty of the Clink in Southwark.

The assessment of his personal estate (goods, chattels, cash, leases, etc.) at £5 means very little. He was clearly quite a wealthy man by 1597, in a position to buy a large house in Stratford and to attract requests for substantial loans from his friends.[1] The tax records are valuable for the Shakespearian biographer as they provide the only evidence as to where he was living between 1596 and 1600. In 1596 or, at the latest February 1597, he was a parishioner of St Helen's Bishopgate, conveniently close to Shoreditch where the Lord Chamberlain's company performed. By the time the commissioners came to look for him in 1597, he had moved away. In 1598-9 he was found by the authorities living somewhere in Surrey; in the next year he was certainly in the liberty of the Clink in Southwark. It is generally assumed that he moved south of the river when his company transferred to the Globe Theatre. The 1596 writ of attachment (document 7) supports the idea that he moved to Southwark in that year as it is addressed to the sheriff of Surrey and Sussex. By 1604 he had moved to the parish of St Olave in the northwest corner of the city, as is evident from the records of the law suit *Belott* v. *Mountjoy*.

10. Entry on the main account of the Exchequer (Pipe Roll) of Shakespeare's tax debt of 13s. 4d., 1599-1600 (E 372/445 m. Residuum Sussex). Translation: William Shakespeare in the parish of St Helen's, 13s. 4d. of the first entire subsidy granted in the said thirty ninth year |of the reign of Queen Elizabeth| which is required upon the same there.

In 1909 Professor Charles Wallace discovered twentysix documents among the records of the Court of Requests in the case of *Belott* v. *Mountjoy*; Shakespeare's name occurs twentyfour times and his signature once. In 1604, it appears, Shakespeare was lodging in the house of Christopher Mountjoy, a Huguenot maker of fashionable headdresses, at the corner of Silver Street and Mugwell (afterwards Monkwell Street) near St Olave's church in Cripplegate. Mountjoy's daughter, Mary, and his apprentice, Stephen Belott, who also lived in the house,

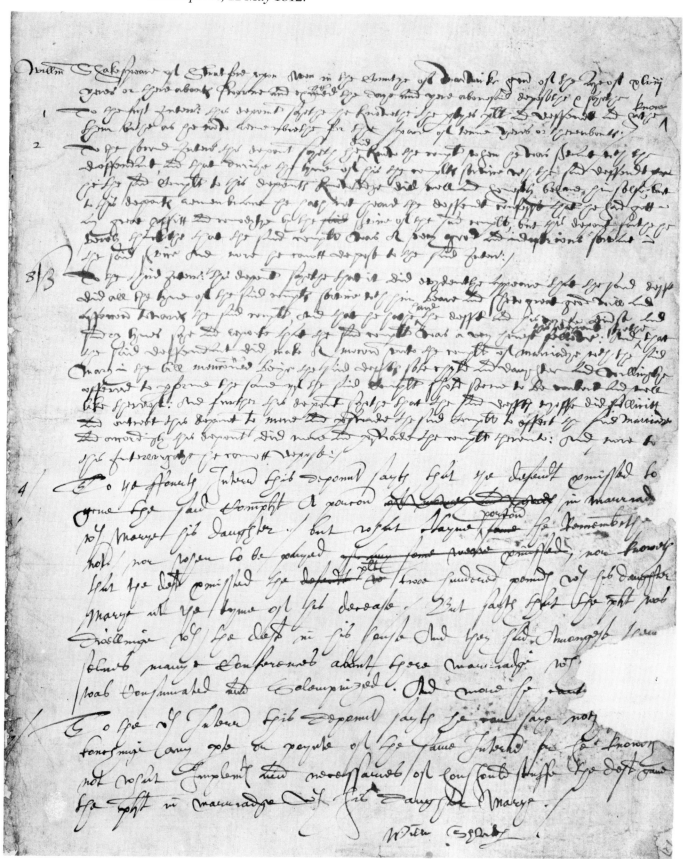

11. The case of Stephen Belott versus Christopher Mountjoy (REQ 4/1), deposition of William Shakespeare, 11 May 1612.

were encouraged by Shakespeare to get married, which they did on 19 November. The outcome was not happy: Stephen and his father-in-law quarrelled about the non-payment of Mary's dowry. According to Belott, Mountjoy had promised him £60 on the marriage and a further sum of £200 to be left in his will. Instead, Mountjoy had given him only £10 and some 'household stuffe'. By 1612 matters had come to a head and Belott, fearing that he would be cut out of Mountjoy's will, went to court.

Shakespeare's role as go-between is decribed by the witnesses who were called to give evidence. Joan Johnson, a servant in the household, 'Remembreth the def|endan|t did send and perswade one Mr Shakespeare that laye in the house to perswade the pl|ain|t|iff| to the same Marriadge'. Daniel Nicholas said that Mountjoy 'did move the pl|ain|t|iff| by him the said Shakespeare to have |a| marriadge betweene his daughter Marye Mountioye |and| the pl|ain|t|iff|.' Shakespeare's own deposition survives in the form of written answers to a series of questions. He stated that he had known both parties in the case 'as he now remembrethe for the space of tenne yeres or thereabouts' and that 'duringe the tyme of his the compl|ainan|ts service wth the said deffend|an|t' Belott did 'well and honestly behave himselfe'. The dramatist further recalled that Mountjoy had often spoken well of his apprentice and 'did make A moc|i|on unto the compl|ainan|t of marriadge wth the said Mary [Mountjoy] ... And further this dep|on|ent sayethe that the said deff|endan|ts wyeffe did sollicitt and entreat this dep|on|ent to move and perswade the said Compl|ainan|t to effect the said marriadge and accordingly this dep|on|ent did move and perswade the compl|ainan|t thereunto'. He deposed that Mountjoy had promised 'A porc|i|on *of monie and goodes* (struck through) in marriad|ge| wth Marye his daughter' but could not remember the amount. He did not know anything about a promise to pay £200 at Mountjoy's death or what household goods had been given to Belott at the time of his marriage. At the end of the deposition the dramatist's signature appears in the contracted form 'Willm Shakp'. The outcome of the case was unsatisfactory for Belott. The Court of Requests referred the matter to the overseers and elders of the French church in London who decided that Mountjoy should pay him twenty nobles (£6 13s. 4d.). A year later the money had not been paid.

Although the evidence in the suit is voluminous and Shakespeare's name occurs many times, the contribution it makes to the story of his life is disappointingly slight. All we learn is that the playwright had known the Mountjoys since 1602, that he got involved in their daughter's marriage plans and that he was a lodger in their house in 1604. Nevertheless, Shakespeare's connection with the Huguenot family has been ridden hard by literary historians. Some have supposed that he remembered his language lessons from Mountjoy when writing the French dialogue in *Henry V.* Professor Wallace believed that the herald Mountjoy who appears in the scenes before and after Agincourt was named after Shakespeare's landlord; this is unlikely as the first reference to *Henry V* in the Stationer's Register is dated August 1600 and predates Shakespeare's arrival in Cripplegate. Moreover the name Mountjoy was the official title for one of the French heralds in the fifteenth century and was used by Holinshed in the *Chronicles* on which Shakespeare's play was based.

The records only give hints about Shakespeare's private life in London; for his professional life there is much more. The first piece of official evidence linking Shakespeare to the theatre comes from 1595 when he was already established as an actor and playwright; he had written *The Comedy of Errors, Titus Andronicus, The Taming of the Shrew, Henry VI, Richard III* and the narrative poems, *Venus and Adonis* and *The Rape of Lucrece.* An account of payments made to Shakespeare and others for acting at court shows him as a member of the company which operated under the patronage of the Lord Chamberlain of the Household, Lord Hunsdon. From then on his life was bound up with the Lord Chamberlain's Company, first in Shoreditch and later at the Globe. The account is for £13 6s. 8d. and £13 13s. 4d. paid by the Treasurer of the Chamber (who was responsible for disbursements in the royal household) to William Kempe, William Shakespeare and Richard Burbage for two comedies or interludes performed before the queen at Christmas 1594, on St Stephen's Day (26 December) and Innocents' Day (28 December). The second date is usually assumed to be a mistake for the 27th as, according to another account, the Lord Admiral's Men were performing at court on the 28th and the Lord Chamberlain's Men are known to have been at Gray's Inn putting on *The Comedy of Errors*. Shakespeare's two colleagues named in the account are the leading tragic actor, Richard Burbage, and the comedian and dancer William Kempe. Other members of the company at this period were Augustine Phillips, Thomas Pope, William Sly, John Heminges and George Bryan.

12. Account of payments by the Treasurer of the Chamber, 1595 (E 351/542 m.207d.), 'To Will[i]am Kempe Will[i]am Shakespeare & Richarde Burbage servauntes to the Lord Chamberleyne upon the Councelles warr[an]t dated at Whitehall xv^{to} Martii 1594 for twoe severall Comedies or Enterludes shewed by them before her ma[jes]tie in Christmas tyme laste paste. Viz. upon St Stephens daye & Innocentes daye xiii li. vi s. viii d. and by waye of her ma[jes]t[i]es Rewarde vi li. xiii s. iiii d. in all xx li.'.

Between 1595 and 1601 Shakespeare produced many plays and the company flourished, moving to a fine new playhouse on Bankside and thriving on competition with its rival company, the Admiral's Men. In 1601 Shakespeare and the others found themselves in a dangerous situation which could have been disastrous not only for their company but for the theatre in general. Queen Elizabeth's former favourite, the Earl of Essex, was planning a rebellion and, as part of the propaganda campaign, the Lord Chamberlain's Men were persuaded to put on a performance of *Richard II,* a play about the deposing of a monarch. The company was paid an extra forty shillings and the curtain went up on 7 February, the day before the abortive rising. The players were examined during the trial of the rebels, the deposition of Augustine Phillips is given as document 13. One of the rebels, Sir Gilly Meyrick faced a number of charges including the procurement of the performance of *Richard II,* and was executed but the players were forgiven. There were no reprisals, which is surprising when one considers that four years earlier a production of the seditious *Isle of Dogs* so disturbed the Privy Council that all theatres were ordered to be closed.

86. 58 139

128 148

153

The ex|aminati|on of Augustyn Phillypps
servant unto the L|ord| Chamberlyne
and one of hys players taken
the xviii[th] of Februarii 1600 upon
hys oth.
He sayeth that on Fryday last was senyght or Thursday, S|i|r Charles Percy S|i|r Jostlyne
Percy and the L|ord| Montegle wth some thre more spake to some of the players in the presens
of this exa|minant| to have the play of the deposyng and kyllyng of Kyng Rychard the Second
to be played the *next* (struck through) *Satedy* (interlined) *day* (struck through) *next* (inter-
lined) promysyng to geve them xls more then their ordynary to play yt. Wher thys exa|minant|
and hys freindes were determyned to have playd some other play holdyng that play of Kyng
Rychard to be so old & so long out of use as that they shold have small or no cumpney
|company| at yt. But at their request this exa|minant| and hys freindes were content to play yt
the Saterday and hadd their xls. more then their ordynary for yt and so played y[t] accordyngly
Augustine Phillipps
(signed)

ex|aminatus| per
Jo|hn| Popham
Edmund Anderson
Edward Fenner

opposite   *13. Examination of Augustine Phillips before John Popham, Lord Chief Justice,
Edmund Anderson, Chief Justice of Common Pleas and Edward Fenner, Judge of the
Queen's Bench, concerning the performance of* Richard II *before Essex's rebellion, 18 Febru-
ary 1601 (SP 12/278/85).*

The company does not seem to have suffered in any way from its political involvement and when James I came to the throne in 1603 it was taken into royal patronage within ten days of the king's arrival in London. As the King's Players the company was now firmly established as the leading troupe in the country. Of the players named in the letters patent Shakespeare, Burbage, Phillips, Heminges, Condell, Sly, Armin and Cowley had all been members of the Lord Chamberlain's Men. The only notable absentee was Thomas Pope who was, by then, near his death. Lawrence Fletcher who heads the list had probably not been a member of the company but had acted before King James in Scotland.

14. *Enrolment of letters patent authorizing Shakespeare and his companions to perform plays throughout the realm, 19 May 1603 (C 66/1608 m.4), 'Wee . . . licence and aucthorize theise our servaunts Lawrence Fletcher Will[ia]m Shakespeare Richard Burbage Augustyne Phillippes John Hemings Henrie Condell Will[ia]m Sly Rob[er]t Armyn Richard Cowly and the rest of theire Assosiates freely to use and exercise the Arte and faculty of playinge Comedies Tragedies Histories Enterludes Moralls pastoralls Stageplaies and suche others like as theie have alreadie studied or hereafter shall use or studie aswell for the recreation of our lovinge Subiects as for our Solace and pleasure when wee shall thincke good to see them duringe our pleasure . . . aswell within theire nowe usuall howse called the Globe within our County of Surrey as alsoe within anie towne halls or moute halls or other conveniente places within the lib[er]ties and freedome of anie other Cittie universitie towne or Boroughe whatsoever'.*

When the king's coronation, delayed by an outbreak of plague, finally took place the following year, the King's Men named in the letters patent were each issued with four and a half yards of scarlet cloth for their livery. There is no evidence that the players took part in the coronation ceremonials; grants of red cloth were commonly made to crown servants on important royal occasions.

15. Account of Sir George Hume, Master of the Great Wardrobe, showing a grant of scarlet-red cloth to Shakespeare and his companions for the king's coronation procession, 15 March 1604 (LC 2/4(5) p.78).

The King's Men did take part in one major event in 1604. An account of the Treasurer of the Chamber records payment made to them for attending on the Spanish ambassador at Somerset House in August. The ambassador was in London to negotiate a peace treaty. Although Shakespeare is not named, it is a reasonable assumption that he was among the ten 'fellowes' who appeared with Phillips and Heminges.

16. Account of payment to the King's Men for attendance on the Spanish ambassador 9-27 August 1604 (AO 1/388/41).

17. Will of Augustine Phillips, 4 May 1605 (PROB 11/105 s.31), 'Item I give and bequeath unto and amongest the hired men of the company w[hi]ch I am of w[hi]ch shall be at the tyme of my decease the somme of five poundes of lawfull money of England to be equally distributed amongeste them. Item I give and bequeath to my fellowe William Shakespeare a xxx s. peece in gould To my fellow Henry Condell one other xxx s. peece in gould. To my servaunte Christopher Besone xxx s. in gould, To my fellow Lawrence Fletcher xx s. in gould, To my fellow Rob[er]te Armyne xx s. in gould To my fellow Richard Cowley xx s. in gould To my fellow Allexander Cooke xx s. in golde, To my fellow Nicholas Tooley xx s. in gould.'

The company was a close-knit group and some idea of the family feeling which prevailed at the Globe is given by the will of Shakespeare's old associate Augustine Phillips, who died in 1605.

James I was fond of theatrical entertainment and the King's Men are known to have performed at court at least 107 times between the grant of letters patent in 1603 and Shakespeare's death in 1616. One of the celebrated Revels' Accounts (document 18) lists the plays performed at court in 1605. The Master of the Revels was the official responsible for the stage and properties needed for masques and plays put on at court; he was also the censor and issued licences for public shows. The document is in the usual form of draft account, detailing the expenses of the office, which was held at that time by Edmund Tylney. The first item is a statement that Tylney had received an advance or imprest of £100 for the current year and a payment of £66 9s. 10d. owed to him from the previous year's account. At the end is a statement of balance due and a certificate signed by Thomas Flemyng, Auditor of the Imprests, to the effect that Tylney had taken the ordinary accountant's oath. The draft was sent into the Exchequer where it was checked, recast into the formal Auditor's Declared Account and signed by the Auditor and one of the Barons of the Exchequer. The feature of interest in his draft account is the appended list of plays, giving the titles of the pieces and their authors' names, among them 'Shaxberd'. This is the only formal official contemporary reference to Shakespeare as a playwright rather than an actor; as well as being the earliest known reference to *Othello* and *Measure for Measure*. As such it is a key piece of evidence for the dating and authorship of these plays, but unfortunately its reputation is tarnished.

For many years the account was regarded as suspect. It was first brought to light by Peter Cunningham in the Audit Office and was printed by him in 1842. When the Audit Office records were transferred to the Public Record Office, Cunningham kept his prize discovery and later tried to sell it to the British Museum, with some other Shakespeare accounts. The Master of the Rolls impounded them and a private dealer, learning what had happened, handed over some documents he had bought from Cunningham. The mystery surrounding these events and the unusual appearance of the accounts led many people to think that Cunningham had forged them. The validity of the 1605 document was apparently settled for all time earlier in this century by the writer, Ernest Law and A.E. Stamp, Deputy Keeper of Public Records. Law pointed out that a transcript of the account had been shown to the Shakespeare scholar Edmund Malone long before it had fallen into Cunningham's hands. Stamp compared the supposed forgery with the Auditor's Declared Account and found that, although the latter was in a condensed form, which did not mention the plays, the balances and totals tallied. Moreover, the Declared Account is written in the same hand as the certificate at the end of Tylney's account and both documents bear the signature of Thomas Flemyng. Microscopic examination showed that the whole document is written in the same ink, a type containing a large quantity of gum; this disposed of the theory that the passages relating to Shakespeare had been written into an otherwise genuine record.

The variant 'Shaxberd' is unique among the hundred or more known spellings of the name, although the forms 'Shaxber' and 'Shaxbere' are not uncommon. The suggestion has been made that it was the work of an official newly arrived from Scotland with James I who spelt the name as a Scot might pronounce it. There is no evidence to support this interesting theory.

The account for 1611-12 (document 19) is another Cunningham discovery and has a similar history. A curious sign in the shape of a sickle occurs over a number of words, in particular where a second 'l' has been inserted in the word 'called'. This was regarded as the work of a forger until A.E. Stamp compared it with some letters written by Sir George Buc, then Master of the Revels, in his own hand, and found the sickle sign over his double 'l's'.

18. Account of Edmund Tylney, Master of the Revels, for the year 1 November 1604 to 31 October 1605 (AO 3/908/13), showing performances of plays by 'Shaxberd': Othello (*'The Moor of Venis'*), The Merry Wives of Windsor, Measure for Measure, The Comedy of Errors (*'The plaie of Errors'*), Love's Labours Lost. *Reference to* Henry V *and* The Merchant of Venice, *is made on the next sheet, not reproduced above.*

The names, of the playes And by what Company played
them hearafter ffollowethe: As Also what Maskes, and Triumphs
att the Tilte were presented before the kinge wer in this year 1611

By the Kings players: **Hallomas**, Nyght was presented att Whithall before ye kinge ma^{tie}
A play Called the Tempest:

The Kings players: **The 5.th of nouember**: A play Called ye winters nigtte Tayles

The Kings players: **On St Stiuenes** night A play Called Kinge no kinge & kinge aty king

The Queens players: **St John**, night A play Called the City Gallant.

The princes players: **The sunday**, ffollowinge A play Called the Almanak

The Kings Players: **On neweres**, night A play Called the Twines Tragedie
And kinge att the king
The Childern of whitfriers ye Sunday ffollowing A play Called Cupids Reueng
This day the Kinge prince
wth diuer of his Noblemen **Twelfe**, night The princes Mask performed by Gentelmen of his tys
did run att ye Ring for
a prize.

By the Queens players **The sunday** ffollowinge att Grnwidg before ye Quten and
and the Kings men the prince was playd the Siluer Aieda and ye next nigt following Lucre

By the Quens players **Candelmas** night A play Called Tu Coque

By the Kings players **Shroue sunday**: A play Called the Noblman

By the Duck of yorks **Shroue Munday** A play Called Hmens Haliday
Players

By the Laydy Elizabeths **Shroue Teuesday** A play Called the proud Mayds Tragedie
Players

On the 24:^{tv} day of marche Being the Kings Ma^{tis} day
of his Entrie to the Croune of England was performed at ye
Tilt A Triumph.

The account refers to two Shakespeare plays, *The Winter's Tale* and *The Tempest.* The astrologer Simon Forman mentions in his *Booke of Plaies and Notes thereof* that *The Winter's Tale* was performed on 15 May 1611 at the Globe but the account is the earliest firm reference to *The Tempest.*

The last document in this section gives a useful summary of the ownership of the theatres used by the King's Men. The first permanent theatre in London was built in Shoreditch in 1576 by James Burbage who had originally been the chief actor to the Earl of Leicester. Others soon appeared: the Curtain, also in Shoreditch, the Playhouse in Newington Butts, the Rose and Swan on Bankside. Shakespeare's company played in the Theatre until the lease expired and Burbage died in 1597. His son, Cuthbert had difficulty renewing the lease; the ground landlord offered unacceptable terms and planned to demolish the building in order to recover and re-use the materials. The chief shareholders of the company agreed to establish a new playhouse and the Theatre was torn down by Cuthbert Burbage and his brother, Richard, the tragic actor, under the cover of darkness, and the timber and other materials were carried over the river to Bankside. By July 1599 the actors, who had been playing in the Curtain in the meantime, were able to open in their new theatre, the Globe. Although the removal of the building material was permitted under the terms of the lease, the landlord was enraged and took legal action.

The Globe was owned and operated by a syndicate who held a lease from the ground landlord, Sir Nicholas Brend. The shareholders were the Burbage brothers, Shakespeare, Augustine Phillips, Thomas Pope, John Heminges and William Kempe. Initially the Burbages held half the shares, while Shakespeare and the others had a tenth each. The value of these shareholdings varied as members left or new ones were admitted to the syndicate. The King's Men used the theatre until 1644 when the lease expired and it was demolished. In 1613 the building was burnt down when the canon fire heralding the entrance of Henry VIII onto the stage ignited the thatch. The shareholders had to put up £50-£60 to rebuild the theatre and it has been suggested that Shakespeare took this opportunity to sell his interest in the enterprise.

The Globe was an open-air theatre, only suitable for the summer. The company took over the smaller, more select Blackfriars theatre for winter performances; it was enclosed so there were no problems with the weather and plays were acted by candlelight. The syndicate which took over the theatre in 1608 comprised the Burbage brothers, Shakespeare, John Heminges, Henry Condell, William Sly and Thomas Evans; each shareholder was responsible for one seventh of the rent of £40 a year.

The document reproduced here is one of the records of a dispute which arose in 1635 (Shakespeare had been dead for nineteen years) between the members of the King's Men and the partners who owned the Globe and the Blackfriars theatres. Three of the players, Thomas Pollard, Heliard Swanston and Robert Benfield, petitioned the Lord Chamberlain, asking that the partners be compelled to sell some shares to the actors so their income should be augmented. The answer of Cuthbert Burbage, his son, William, and his sister-in-law, Winifred, explains how James Burbage had been 'the first builder of Playhowses', how the Globe was built and how James had purchased the land on which the Blackfriars theatre stood 'at extreame rates & made it into a playhouse with great charge and troble'. It tells the story of how the theatre was leased to Henry Evans who had the Children of the Chapel acting there until they were suppressed in 1608, when the King's Men took it over. As far as the petitioners' claim was concerned, Burbage pointed out that 'The Players that lived in those first times had onely the profitts arising from the dores, but now the players receave all the commings in at the dores to themselves & halfe the Galleries from the Houskeepers [shareholders]'.

20. The answer of Cuthbert Burbage, his son, William, and his brother's wife, Winifred, to the petition by Robert Benfield, Heliard Swanston and Thomas Pollard to the Lord Chamberlain of the Household, 1635 (LC 5/133 p.50), 'We … built the Globe …& to o[u]r selves wee ioyned those deserveing men Shakspere Hemings, Condall, Philips and others partners'. At Blackfriars the Burbages 'soe purchased the lease remaining from Evans with o[u]r money & placed men Players, which were Hemings, Condall, Shakspeare etc'.

III Shakespeare in Stratford

Prospero's farewell in *The Tempest* has been seen as Shakespeare's final curtain. He wrote few plays after 1610; his last was probably a collaboration with Fletcher on *The Noble Kinsman,* which is thought to have been written in 1613. The last few years of his life, it is assumed, were spent with his family in Stratford and he died there in 1616.

Shakespeare had retained his Stratford connections throughout his life, keeping in touch with friends as is clear from his will, taking neighbours to court and buying property there. Nothing is known about his relations with his family during the years he spent in London. He presumably supported them, but did he go home when his young son, Hamnet, was dying in 1596 or when his daughter, Susanna, married in 1607? Did Ann Hathaway ever go to the Globe?

He bought a fine house for them in Stratford, New Place, at the time when he was failing to pay his London taxes. It was a fifteenth-century property, a 'pretty house of brick and timber', built by a member of the Clopton family at the corner of Chapel Street and Chapel Lane. In 1563 it passed to a wealthy business man, William Bott, who sold it in 1567 to William Underhill, the father of the man from whom Shakespeare bought it in 1597. The younger Underhill was a prominent Stratford figure and the escheator for Warwickshire and Leicestershire. The legality of the transaction was upset by a tragedy in the Underhill family. On 7 July 1597, only two months after selling the house, William Underhill died, poisoned by his son, Fulke. The boy was executed and his conviction may have called into question Shakespeare's title to the property. The Underhill estate escaped forfeiture to the crown and descended to the second son, Hercules, who concluded a further agreement with Shakespeare when he came of age in 1602. Shakespeare's title to the house was established beyond dispute.

New Place; the frontage. The only surviving pictorial record of New Place as Shakespeare knew it. It was entirely rebuilt in 1702. (BL, MS, Portland Loan 29/246 p18). Reproduced by kind permission of His Grace the Duke of Portland.

Document 21 is part of the record of the 1597 conveyance. The house was transferred by the legal process known as a Final Concord or Fine. This involved a fictitious legal action in the Court of Common Pleas in which the purchaser (in this case Shakespeare) brought a suit against the vendor (Underhill), laying claim to the property in question. With the court's permission, the vendor came to an agreement with the purchaser in which he admitted the latter's claim: Underhill admitted that Shakespeare owned New Place. The agreement between the two parties was known as the Concord. The text of the agreement was written out three times on a single skin of parchment and then divided along indented lines to produce three copies. Each party kept a copy, called an Indenture and the third copy, the Foot, was kept by the court together with the Concord. The 1597 Fine for New Place describes the property as comprising one messuage, two barns and two gardens with appurtenances in Stratford. The 1602 conveyance, also by Fine, mentions two orchards in addition. The latter document gives Shakespeare the title of 'gentleman', a dignity accorded him in recognition of the arms he had acquired on the death of his father in 1601. In both conveyances the purchase price is given as £60, but this is of little significance as valuations in Fines are normally fictitious.

21. Foot of Fine recording the sale of New Place to Shakespeare, 1597 (CP 25(2)/237, Easter 39 Eliz. I), Shakespeare's copy of the deed is preserved in the Shakespeare Birthplace Trust Museum.

Over the next few years Shakespeare, who, according to Alexander Pope, wrote for 'gain not glory', acquired further property. His father's death in 1601 brought him the ownership of the house in Henley Street, the Birthplace, where his mother probably lived until her death seven years later. In 1602 he bought a cottage near to New Place, in Chapel Lane. There has been some speculation as to why he did this; the property was not valuable enough to have had attractions as an investment so it is thought that he wanted it to provide accommodation for a servant or perhaps some member of the family. The cottage and garden were an outlying part of the manor of Rowington and Shakespeare acquired them by the normal process used in the conveyance of land held by the tenure known as copyhold: the vendor surrendered the property to the lord of the manor and a grant of admittance was made to the purchaser. A copy of the entry on the Rowington manor court roll recording the entry of the surrender by Walter Getley and the regrant to Shakespeare survives in the Birthplace Trust Museum. In the Public Record Office there is the record of a survey of Rowington made two years after the purchase when the property reverted to the crown on the death of the widow of the lord of the manor, Ambrose, Earl of Warwick.

22. Survey of the manor of Rowington, 24 October 1604 (E 178/4661), 'Will[ia]m Shakespere lykewise holdeth there one Cottage & one garden by estimation a quarter of one acre and payeth Rent yeerlye ii s. vi d.'

In the same year that he bought the cottage he paid £320 to John Combe and the latter's uncle, William, for 107 acres of arable land in Old Stratford with right of common for sheep, horses and cattle. John Combe was the richest man in Stratford and well known as a money lender. His unpopularity in the town was probably the source of the story (which appears in many forms) which tells how Shakespeare composed a vicious epitaph for the old man, describing him as the devil's son. In fact the two men must have been close friends as Combe left Shakespeare £5 in his will and the playwright left Combe's nephew, Thomas, his sword.

23. Will of John Combe, proved in the Prerogative Court of Canterbury, 1615 (PROB 11/126 s.118), 'to mr. William Shackspere five poundes'.

Before his death Shakespeare made two further property investments: in 1605 he paid £440 for tithes in the Stratford area which brought him an income of £60 a year and in 1613 he bought a house in Blackfriars, a tenement 'over a great gate'. The deed of purchase of the tithes is now in the Birthplace Trust Museum, the indenture of bargain and sale for the Blackfriars property is in the Guildhall Library; a mortgage deed by which £60 was raised to pay for the property is in the British Library.

IV Shakespeare's Will and Signatures

As the most personal and the richest in biographical detail of the surviving Shakespeare documents, his will has been the subject of intense critical scrutiny. Its innocent legal phrases have triggered the wildest flights of scholarly fancy; every pen stroke, every blot, every fold in the paper is fraught with significance. A detailed study of the provisions of the will made by B. Roland Lewis earlier this century led him to proclaim that the 'essential spirit of Shakespeare is found in his will . . . It more than any one thing mirrors his personality. His business astuteness and the hopes and ambitions of his busy life here find virile and definite expression'.[1] Probably nearer the truth is the opinion of Joseph Green, the Stratford antiquarian who was the first to look among the records of the probate court for the will: 'the Legacies and Bequests therein are undoubtedly as he intended; but the manner of introducing them, appears to me so . . . absolutely void of the least particle of that Spirit which Animated Our great Poet'.[2] Shakespeare had no telling final words for his audience; his last wishes were dictated to a local lawyer, Francis Collins, who had drawn up the tithe purchase document and whatever intensity of feeling there may have been in the words he spoke, however, beautifully expressed, there is no hint of it in the written version. It is a standard legal document and, with one or two exceptions, the provisions are exactly those one would expect from a fairly wealthy small-town gentleman. There is nothing remarkable about the language used in the will - no other sixteenth or seventeenth century poet is known to have broken into blank verse on his deathbed - but its austerity is a disappointment. There is no reference to a 'good and faithful servant', a 'sweet grandchild', an 'obedient daughter' or a 'loving wife'. The impersonal drafting may be ascribed entirely to Francis Collins or it may be partly a reflection of Shakespeare's own legal knowledge; he was almost certainly familiar with the work of Henry Swinburne, the author of the leading testamentary manual of the day.[3]

According to a tradition, repeated in John Ward's diary fifty years after the event, Shakespeare died of a fever which he caught following a 'merry party' with Ben Jonson and some other friends. His burial entry in the Stratford parish register is dated 25 April 1616. It is assumed that at the time, he was living with his wife in New Place. His only son was dead and his two daughters were married; Susanna, the elder, had made a good match with the physician John Hall, and had given Shakespeare a granddaughter, Elizabeth; Judith's recent marriage to a local vintner, Thomas Quiney, had started badly. Judith was thirty-one and perhaps short of suitors; Thomas was four years younger. The wedding was on 10 February 1616 and the couple failed to follow the proper procedure and obtain a special licence to marry in Lent. They were excommunicated. On 26 March, a month before Shakespeare's death, his new son-in-law was fined five shillings by the Stratford ecclesiastical court for fornicating with one Margaret Wheeler, who had died in labour with Quiney's child, a fortnight earlier. The shock of the scandal may have hastened Shakespeare's end, but it is more likely that he was already ill as the first draft of his will appears to have been made in January; in the seventeenth century men rarely disposed of their property until they were 'pinched by the messenger of death'.

The will was taken for probate to the Prerogative Court of Canterbury in London, the most senior of a network of church courts handling testamentary business. There John Hall, his son-in-law and one of the executors, took the oath promising to duly administer the estate, on behalf of himself and his wife. This is shown in the probate clause written in Latin on the bottom of the will. The original will was filed and a copy was 'engrossed' on parchment and bound up together with other wills proved that year. The register still survives[4] as does the

[1] See the letter from Richard Quiney asking for £30 now in the Birthplace.

[1] B. Roland Lewis, *The Shakespeare Documents* (1941) II, 471.

[2] S. Schoenbaum, *William Shakespeare: A Documentary Life* (1975), 246

[3] William Rushton, *Shakespeare's Testamentary Language* (1869).

[4] PROB 11/127 s.59.

entry of probate made in the 'Probate Act Book'.[1] There would have been various other documents associated with the grant of probate, possibly affidavits and certainly an inventory of Shakespeare's personal estate, that is to say a list of his household goods, including cash, leases, plate, crops, animals and probably his books and manuscripts. Unfortunately most of the inventories for this date were lost in the Great Fire of 1666. F.J. Furnivall[2] searched through vast quantities of then unsorted Prerogative Court records, leaving in the boxes notes: 'Searched for the inventory of Mr. Shakespeare'.

The original will was written on three pages of paper and there are a number of interlineations and crossings out. It was not unusual for corrected drafts to be submitted for probate; John Combe's will, which was also drawn by Francis Collins, is similar in appearance, though clearly in a different hand. Shakespeare's will was probably written by Collins' clerk; a glance at the lawyer's signature on the last page is enough to show that he did not write it himself. Similarly a comparison of Shakespeare's signatures with the text of the will shows that the will is not holograph, indeed it would be most unusual if it was, no seventeenth-century gentleman, literary or otherwise, penned his own last wishes. The alteration of the date from January to March (at the top of the first page) suggests not only that an earlier draft was made at the beginning of the year, but also that the first page was rewritten. The writing at the bottom of the first page was squeezed in when the second draft was made to save the clerk having to copy out the other two pages as well. The will was almost certainly redrawn so that Shakespeare could alter the provisions for Judith, who married in February 1616; her legacy is dealt with on the first (rewritten) page. The final alterations may have been following the Quiney scandal or the death of Shakespeare's brother-in-law, William Hart, on 17 April.

In the opening phrases of the will, Shakespeare says he is healthy in body and in a fit state to dispose of his property; he commits his soul to God and his body to the earth. This is an absolutely standard preamble which may be found in hundreds of wills of the period. It indicates nothing about his religious proclivities and should not be taken as evidence of his state of health.

The document was attested by the lawyer and four friends: Julius Shawe, from a Henley Street family, Hamnet Sadler, Hamnet Shakespeare's godfather, Robert Whatcote, the chief character witness for Susanna Hall in a slander action in the Worcester Consistory Court, and a John Robinson who has not been identified. It was usual for a man's attorney to be one of the witnesses to the will he had prepared and Collins did not lose his legacy by doing so, neither did Hamnet Sadler. It was not until the Wills' Act of 1837 that beneficiaries were barred from attesting; before then the only people who could not witness a will which benefitted them were the testator's children.[3] There is no particular significance in the number of witnesses, the legal authorities recommended two but many wills of the time have five. The appointment of his elder daughter and her husband as executors is unremarkable; the chief or residuary legatee of a will was usually made responsible for its execution for obvious reasons. Shakespeare named as overseers Collins and Thomas Russell, a member of the local gentry and a literary figure. The appointment of overseers to a will had been common practice since the Middle Ages and was done in the hope that any disputes might be sorted out without recourse to law.

The contents of the will may be summarized quite simply: Shakespeare left the bulk of his estate to his elder daughter, Susanna, and £300 to his younger daughter, Judith. There were a number of small bequests and the devise to Susanna was tied up in such a way as to ensure that the property was kept together and descended in the male line, if there was one. The properties he is known to have held at his death are: New Place, the Birthplace in Henley Street, the tithes he bought in 1605, the land in Old Stratford he bought from the Combes, the cottage near New Place and the house in Blackfriars, in the occupation of a John Robinson. He is thought to have disposed of his theatre shares sometime before he died. The cash bequests in his will amount to about £350. The only personal possessions he makes specific reference to are a large silver gilt bowl (part of his plate), his sword, his clothes and the famous second best bed. Shakespeare's family had certainly improved their financial position since his paternal grandfather, Richard, died fiftyfive years earlier leaving a personal estate valued at £38 7s. 6d.[4]

[1]PROB 8/16.

[2]F.J. Furnivall, 1825-1910, was a noted scholar and editor of literary manuscripts.

[3]Law of Testaments and Last Wills (London, 1744) 7.

[4]Letters of administration of Richard Shakespeare, 1561, Worcester County Record Office.

After the formal preamble Shakespeare started his will with his provision for the newly married Judith. It is evident from the lines that are crossed out at the top of the second page and from the fact that the words 'son-in-law' are struck through in the seventh line of the first page, that in the earlier draft of the will Judith was not the first consideration. It is not unduly fanciful to suppose that after the Quiney scandal his younger daughter was foremost in Shakespeare's thoughts, that he wanted to protect her and, at the same time, make sure that the estate he had built up should be kept together under the wise supervision of Dr John Hall. Judith was to receive £100 as her marriage portion, a very generous sum, and a further £50 on condition she surrendered all rights to the cottage in Chapel Lane, which was to go, with the rest of the real estate, to Susanna. There follows the provision which has been seen as evidence of Shakespeare's deep distrust of Thomas Quiney: Judith was to have a further £150 on condition that her husband settled lands on her to the value of the capital sum. If he failed to do so she was to receive only the interest on the investment (to be made by the executors) and the capital was to pass to her children when she died. Shakespeare probably was worried about Quiney but too much may be made of this; the insistence that a husband should make a settlement on his wife which bore a direct financial correlation to the amount of her dowry was a common feature of seventeenth-century marriage settlements.

Much more interesting is the question of Judith's surrender of her rights in the copyhold cottage as it seems more than likely that she did not have any. When the owner of a copyhold property died the usual procedure was that it was surrendered to the lord of the manor who then regranted it to the heir. If there was no son the property was either divided between the surviving daughters or passed to one of them; either the eldest or the youngest: the rules varied according to the custom of the manor. The custom of Rowington manor, to which the cottage belonged, quite clearly favoured primogeniture: the cottage would have gone to Susanna automatically. The only other person with any rights in the cottage was the widow, Ann Hathaway, who was entitled to 'free bench', which meant she could live in the cottage until she died and would be entered on the manor court roll as copyholder.[1] What then is the explanation of the 'buying off' of Judith's rights and the ommission of any reference to her mother's? The former is probably explained by Shakespeare's anxiety about Judith's husband and possibly by Collins' ignorance of the custom of the manor of Rowington; the final drafting of the will was probably done in a hurry, and he may not have had time to find out. No mention was made of Shakespeare's wife's rights because, presumably, there was no question of her exercising them. She was a simple, loyal, domestic soul perhaps, or was she mentally incapacitated in some way?

The second section of the will is concerned with Shakespeare's sister and her family. He left Joan Hart, who was the only other survivor of the family of eight, £20 and all his clothes and he permitted her to go on living in the family home, the Birthplace, which she did until her death in 1646. Her husband, the hatter William Hart, died just a week before Shakespeare. To his sister's three sons, William, Thomas and Michael, he gave £5 each. Apart from the clothes, the bequests are standard. Most seventeenth century testators made fairly generous gifts to their brothers and sisters, nephews and nieces. The rich garments worn by a man of Shakespeare's status would have been very valuable items (as probate inventories show) and well worth leaving to someone, but it is unusual for men's clothing to be left to a relative of the opposite sex. No other instances have been found in any of a sample of one hundred and fifty wills proved in the Prerogative Court of Canterbury in 1616.[2] One is tempted to make some speculations about Shakespeare's sexual confusion but the reason his doublets and cloaks went to his sister is probably that they were intended for his brother-in-law who had so recently died.

There follows the bequest of his plate to his granddaughter, Elizabeth Hall, referred to later in the will as his niece. There is nothing unusual in the nomenclature; descriptions of relatives were often very vague in seventeenth century wills. When the will was redrafted Elizabeth's name was inserted over the sixth line of the second page after the cancelled section which dealt with the bequests to Judith as they were before she married. It looks as if Shakespeare had originally intended to leave his silver to his younger daughter. When she married Quiney he changed his mind and she got only his large silver gilt bowl.

[1] Survey of the manor of Rowington, E 178/4661.

[2] PROB 11/127.

Shakespeare's gift of £10 to the poor of Stratford was extremely generous. The ancient testamentary custom was that one third of a man's personal estate should be devoted to the cause of buying insurance for a good reception in heaven. Medieval wills contain lavish bequests to the church, and lay charities became the chief recipients after the Reformation. By the early seventeenth century the 'death's part', as it was known, had become a thing of the past and although lip-service was still paid to the idea, even when the court took over the administration of an estate, charity's third was usually given to the widow and children. Men did not stop leaving money to found schools and put out apprentices, but the norm in 1616 wills was a payment of £2 to the local poor, made by yeoman and esquire alike.[1]

There follows a series of minor legacies to friends. Thomas Combe, the nephew of Shakespeare's old friend John, was given his sword. A gentleman would usually leave his sword to his eldest son, but Hamnet Shakespeare was dead. Thomas Russell, the overseer, was left £5 for his pains and the lawyer, Collins, was more generously rewarded with £13 6s. 8d. Overseers and attorneys were often paid in this way. The only hint of theatrical connections is contained in three bequests of 26s. 8d. each to Richard Burbage, John Heminges and Henry Condell to buy mourning rings. Similar sums were allocated to Shakespeare's neighbour, Hamnet Sadler (Richard Tyler is crossed out), William Reynolds, a member of the local gentry, Anthony Nash, a wealthy Stratford landowner, and his brother, John. The practice of leaving money to friends to buy mourning rings was very common until this century.

The creation of an entail on the male line through Susanna or, in default of her heirs, through Judith has been seen as evidence of Shakespeare's virile family pride. There is no doubt that, for whatever reason, Shakespeare was anxious to keep his real estate together, but there is nothing particularly unusual about that and the creation of entails was increasingly popular with the gentry and aristocracy. Did he leave the vast bulk of his considerable estate to his elder daughter because he distrusted his new son-in-law, because he preferred Susanna to Judith, because he did not want the estate broken up or because Elizabeth's birth had proved to him that Susanna and John Hall were capable of producing heirs?

Finally, the widow's miserable souvenir of her absentee husband must be considered. What fun the nineteenth century romantics could have had if only Shakespeare's legacy to his wife had been like that of Thomas Cullwicke of Aldersgate who died in the same year; he left her everything: 'All that I have I give unto the and sorye that it is no more'.[2] As every school child knows, Shakespeare left his wife nothing more than his second best bed, and that appears to have been an afterthought (the interlineation in the middle of the last page of the will). This was no 'affectionate little bequest', neither was it usual for a seventeenth century man, of any rank, to make no overt provision for his wife in his will. Of the sample of 150 wills proved in the same year, mentioned above, about one third of the testators appointed their wives as executrixes and residuary legatees. None left his wife anything as paltry as a second best bed. Bedsteads and bedding *were* without doubt valuable and prized items and they were normally carefully bequeathed, best beds going to wives and eldest sons. The concept of a wife's entitlement to one third of her husband's real estate for life and one third of his personal estate was still very much alive. It was written into marriage settlements and there is constant reference to it in wills of the period. It was not until 1725 that testators were released from their obligation to provide for their widows. The 'verie perfect forme of a Will' given in W. West's *Simboleography,* a contemporary legal manual, gives the occupation of the testator's house to the widow with the profits from his farm and 'also her Thirds out of all my goods' and legacies in recompense for her 'Thirds' and dower. Even unofficial wives had their rights; Thomas Johnes of St Davids left Mary Green, his 'bedfellow', household goods in lieu of her thirds.[3] Ann Shakespeare could have successfully contested the will, but she did not and the assumption is always made that Susanna looked after her and she went on living in New Place until her death.

[1]PROB 11/127.

[2]Will proved 1616, PROB 11/127 s.6.

[3]PROB 11/127 s.6

overleaf   *24. Original will of William Shakespeare, proved June 1616 in the Prerogative Court of Canterbury. PROB 1/4.*

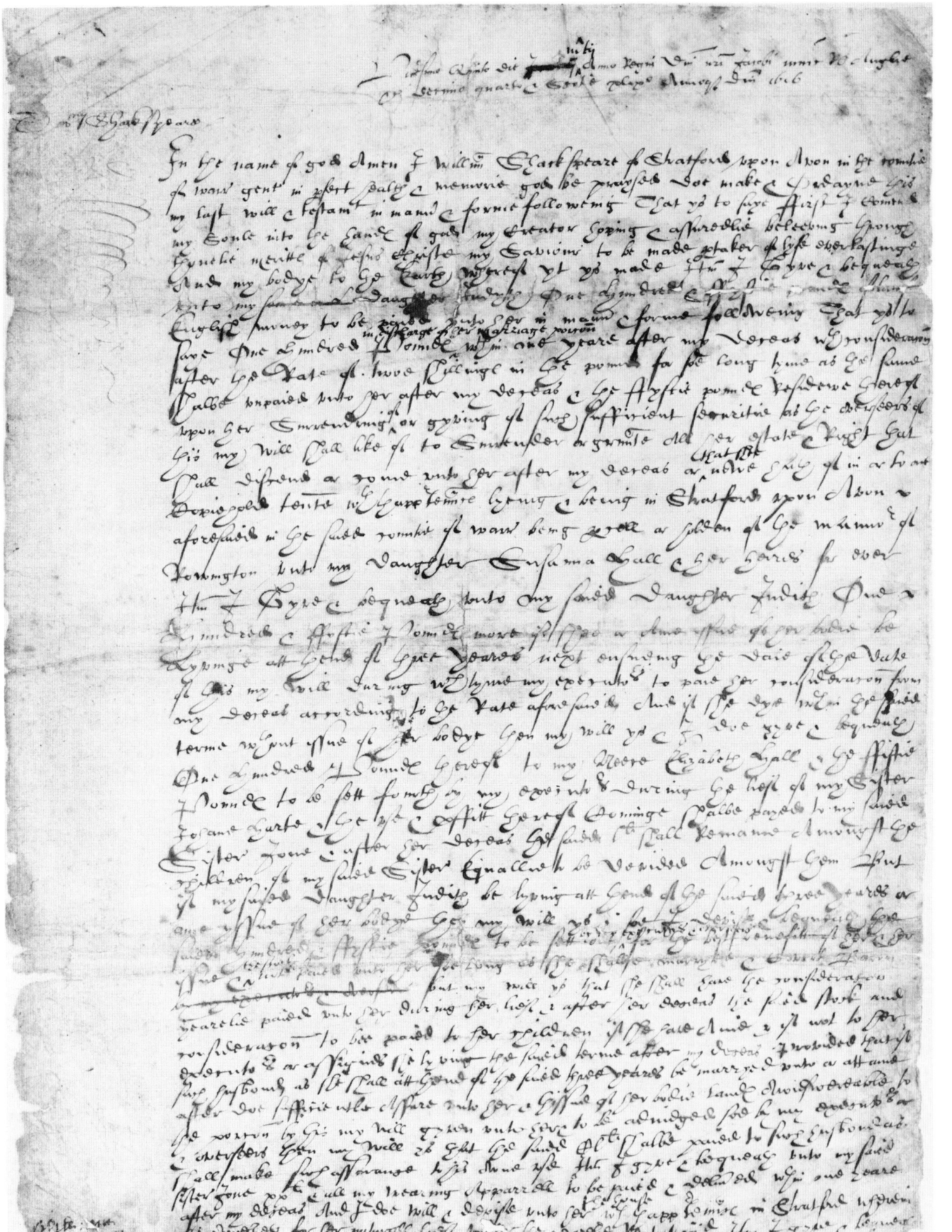

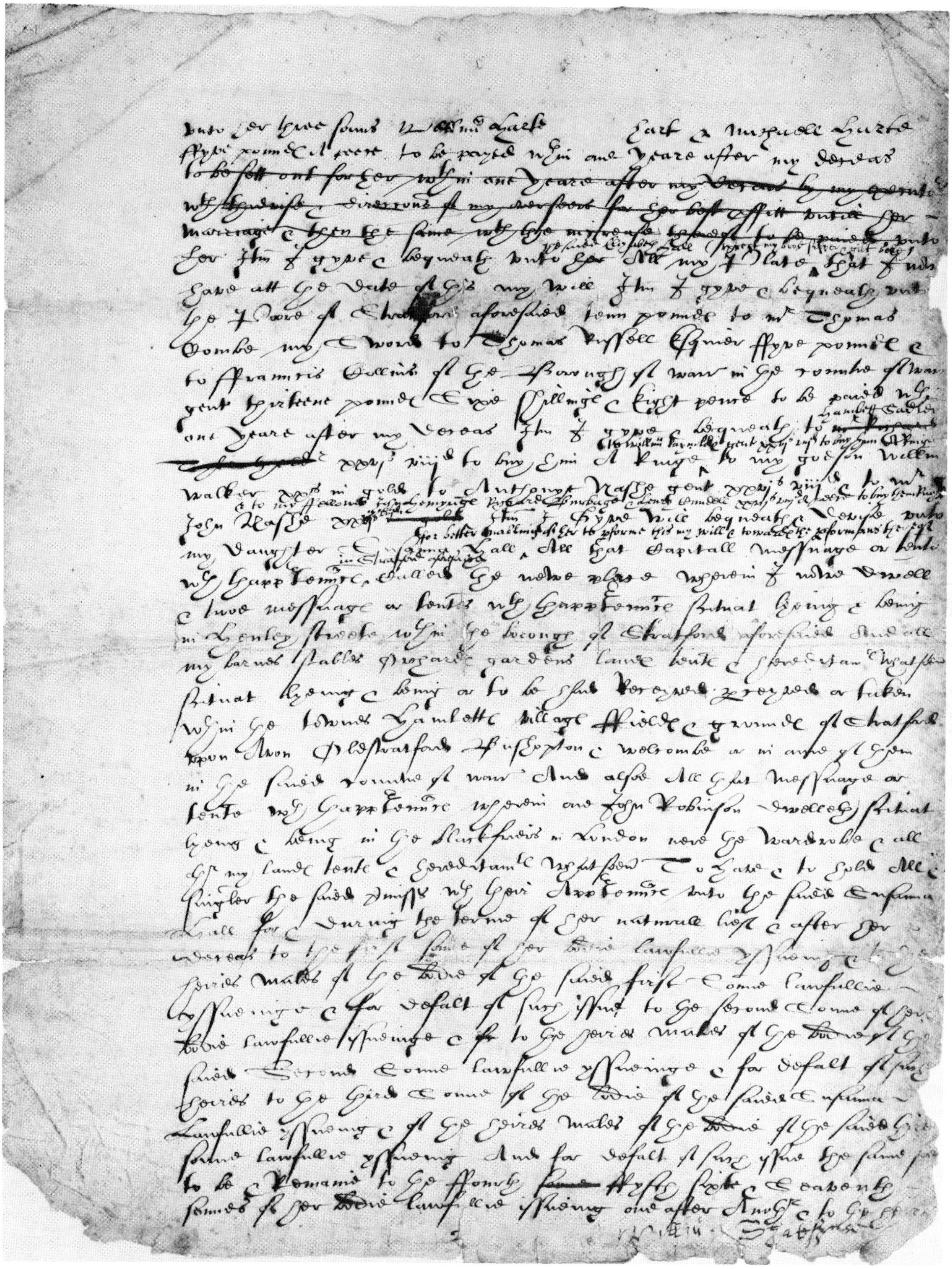

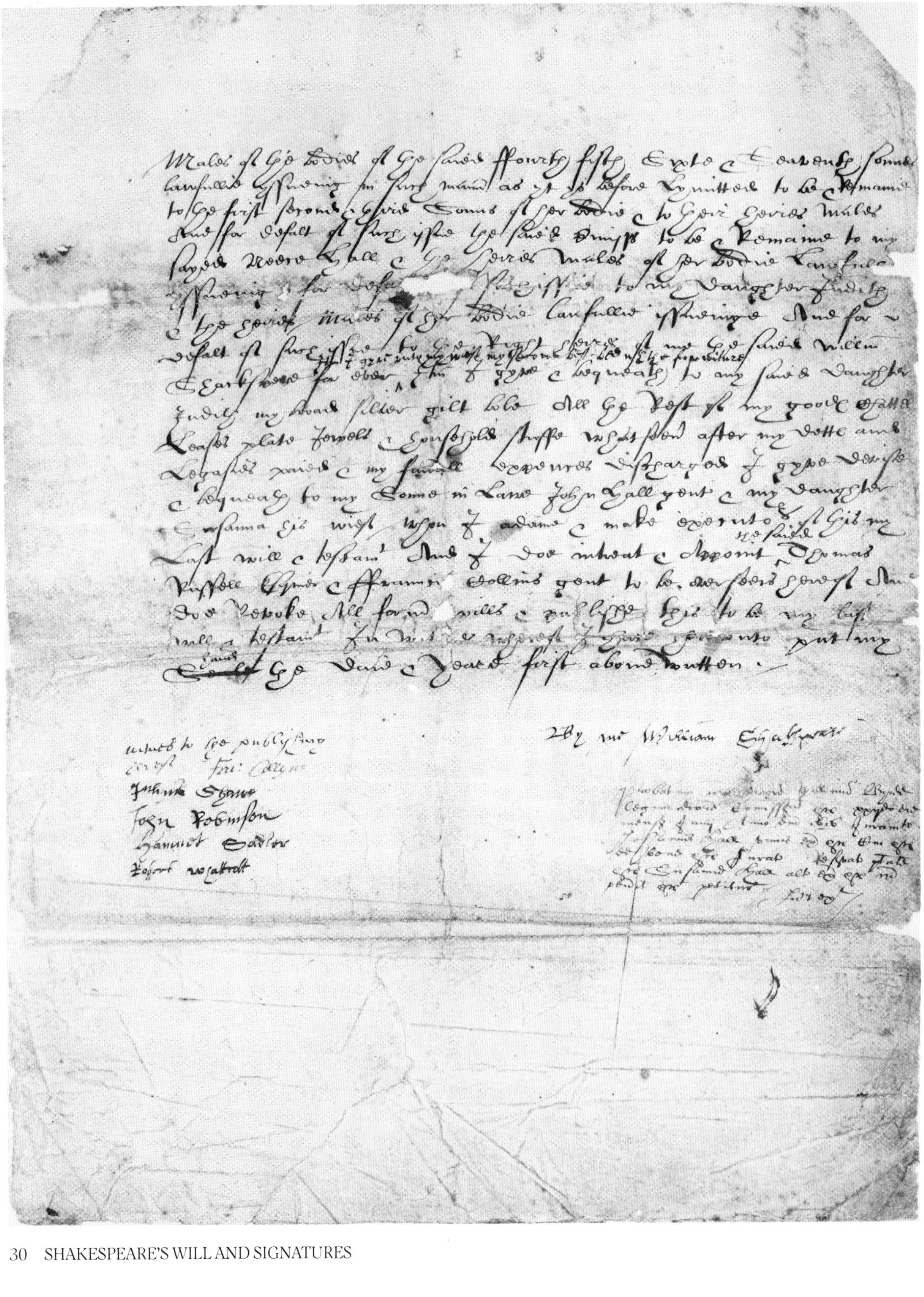

Vicesimo Quinto die *Januarii* (struck through) M|ar|tii Anno Regni D|omi|ni n|ost|ri Jacobi nunc R|egis| Angliae etc. decimo quarto & Scotie xlix° Annoque D|omi|ni 1616

T|estamentum|
W|ille|mi Shackspeare

R|egistretu|r

In the name of god Amen I Willi{a}m Shackspeare of Stratford upon Avon in the countie of Warr' gent in perfect health & memorie god be praysed doe make & Ordayne this my last will & testam|en|{t} in manner & forme followeing That ys to saye first I Comend my Soule into the hands of god my Creator hoping & assuredlie beleeving through thonelie merittes of Jesus Christe my Saviour to be made partaker of lyfe everlastinge And my bodye to the Earth whereof yt ys made. It|e|m I Gyve & bequeath unto my *sonne in L|aw|* (struck through) Daughter Judyth One Hundred & ffyftie pounds of lawfull English money to be paied unto her in manner & forme followeing That ys to saye One Hundred Poundes *in discharge of her marriage porc|i|on* (interlined) within one yeare after my deceas w|i|th considerac|i|on after the Rate of twoe shillinges in the pound for soe long tyme as the same shalbe unpaid unto her after my deceas & the ffyftie pounds Residewe thereof upon her surrendering *of* (interlined) or gyving of such sufficient securitie as the overseers of this my will shall like of to Surrender or graunte All her estate & Right that shall discend or come unto her after my deceas or *that she* (interlined) nowe hath of in or to one Copiehold ten|emen|te with thappertenances lyeing & being in Stratford upon Avon aforesaied in the saied countie of warr' being parcell or holden of the mannor of Rowington unto my daughter Susanna Hall & her heiries for ever. Item I Gyve & bequeath unto my saied Daughter Judyth One Hundred & ffyftie Poundes more if shee or Anie issue of her bodie Lyvinge att thend of three Yeares next ensueing the daie of the date of this my will during which tyme my executors to paie her considerac|i|on from my deceas according to the Rate aforesaied. And if she dye within the saied terme without issue of her bodye then my will ys & I doe gyve & bequeath One Hundred Poundes thereof to my Neece Elizabeth Hall & ffiftie Poundes to be sett fourth by my executors during the lief of my Sister Johane Harte & the use & proffitt thereof Cominge shalbe payed to my saied Sister Jone & after her deceas the saied L{li} shall Remaine Amongst the children of my saied Sister Equallie to be devided Amongst them. But if my saied daughter Judith be lyving att thend of the saied three yeares or anie yssue of her bodye then my will ys & soe I devise & bequeath the saied Hundred & ffyftie poundes to be sett out *by my executors & overseers* (interlined) for the best benefitt of her & her issue and *the stock* (interlined) not *to be* (interlined) paied unto her soe long as she shalbe marryed & Covert Baron *by my executors and overseers* (struck through) but my will ys that she shall have the considerac|i|on yearelie paied unto her during her lief & after her deceas the saied stock and considerac|i|on to bee paied to her children if she have Anie & if not to her executors or Assignes she lyving the saied terme after my deceas provided that if such husbond as she shall att thend of the saied three yeares by marryed unto or attain after doe sufficientlie Assure unto her & thissue of her bodie landes answereable to the porc|i|on gyven unto her & to be adjudged soe by my executors & overseers then my will ys that the saied CL{li} shalbe paied to such husbond as shall make such assurance to his owne use. Item I gyve and bequeath unto my saied sister Jone XX{li} & all my wearing Apparrell to be paied and delivered within one yeare after my deceas. And I doe will & devise unto her *the house* (interlined) with thappurtenances in Stratford wherein she dwelleth for her naturall lief under the yearelie Rent of xiid Item I gyve & bequeath (signed bottom left) William Shake-spere (end of p.1) unto her three sonnes William Harte (name ommitted) Hart & Michaell Harte ffyve poundes A peece to be payed within one yeare after my decease *to be sett out for her within one yeare after my deceas by my executors with thadvise & direccons of my over-seers for her best proffitt untill her marriage & then the same with the increase thereof to be paied unto her* (struck through). Item I gyve & bequeath unto *her* (struck through) *the saied Elizabeth Hall* (interlined) All my Plate *(except my brod silver & gilt bole)* (interlined) that I now have att the date of this my will. Item I gyve & bequeath unto the Poore of Stratford afore-saied tenn poundes; to Mr Thomas Combe my Sword; to Thomas Russell Esquier ffyve poundes & to ffrauncis Collins of the Borough of Warr' in the countie of Warr' gent. thirteene poundes Sixe shillinges & Eight pence to be paied within one yeare after my deceas. Item I gyve & bequeath to *mr. Richard* (struck through) *Hamlett Sadler* (interlined) *Tyler thelder* (struck through) XXVI^s VIII^d to buy him A Ringe; *to William Raynoldes gent. XXVI^s VIII^d to buy him A Ringe* (interlined); to my godson William Walker XX^s in gold; to Anthonye Nashe gent. XXVI^s VIII^d; to mr. John Nashe XXVI^s VIII^d *in gold* (struck through) *& to my ffellowes John Hemynges, Richard Burbage & Henry Cundell XXVI^s VIII^d A peece to buy them Ringes* (interlined). Item I Gyve Will Bequeth & Devise unto my Daughter Susanna Hall *for better enabling of her to performe this my will & towardes the performans thereof* (interlined) All that Capitall Messuage or tenemente with thappurtenances *in Stratford aforesaid* (interlined) called the newe plase wherein I nowe Dwell & two messuages or ten|emen|tes with thappurtenances scituat lyeing & being in Henley Streete within the borough of Stratford aforesaied And all my barnes, stables, Orchardes, gardens, landes, ten|emen|tes & hereditam|en|ts whatsoever scituat lyeing & being or to be had Receyved, perceyved or taken within the townes & Hamletts, villages, ffieldes & groundes of Stratford upon Avon, Oldstratford, Bushopton & Welcombe or in anie of them in the saied countie of warr And alsoe All that Messuage or ten|emen|te with thappurtenances wherein one John Robinson dwelleth, scituat, lyeing & being in the blackfriers in London nere the Wardrobe & all other my landes ten|emen|tes & hereditam|en|tes whatsoever. To Have & to hold All & sing|u|ler the saied premisses with their Appurtenances unto the saied Susanna Hall for & during the terme of her naturall lief & after her deceas to the first sonne of her bodie lawfullie yssueing & to the heiries Males of the bodie of the saied first Sonne lawfullie yssueinge & for defalt of such issue to the second Sonne of her bodie lawfullie issueinge & *of* (struck through) to the heires Males of the bodie of the saied Second Sonne lawfullie yssueinge & for defalt of such heires to the third Sonne of the bodie of the saied Susanna Lawfullie yssueing & of the heires Males of the bodie of the saied third sonne lawfullie yssueing And for defalt of such issue the same soe to be & Remaine to the ffourth, *sonne* (struck through) ffyfth, sixte & Seaventh sonnes of her bodie lawfullie issueing one after Another & to the heires (signed bottom right) William Shakspere (end of p.2) Males of the bodies of the saied ffourth, fifth, Sixte & Seaventh sonnes lawfullie yssueing in such manner as yt ys before Lymitted to be & Remaine to the first, second & third Sonns of her bodie & to their heires males. And for defalt of such issue the saied premisses to be & Remaine to my sayed Neece Hall & the heires Males of her bodie Lawfull|ie| yssueing for defa|ult of| (page damaged) such iss|u|e to my daughter Judith & the heires Males of her bodie lawfullie issueinge. And for defalt of such issue to the Right heires of me the saied Will|ia|m Shackspere for ever. *Item I gyve unto my wief my second best bed with the furniture* (interlined); Item I gyve & bequeath to my saied daughter Judith my broad silver gilt bole. All the Rest of my goodes Chattel|s|, Leases, plate, Jewels & household stuffe whatsoever after my dettes and Legasies paied & my funerall expences discharged, I gyve devise & bequeath to my Sonne in Lawe John Hall gent. & my daughter Susanna his wief whom I ordaine & make executors of this my Last will & testam|en|t. And I doe intreat & Appoint *the saied* (interlined) Thomas Russell Esquier & ffraunci|s| Collins gent. to be overseers hereof And doe Revoke All former wills and publishe this to be my last will & testam|en|t. In Wit|n|es whereof I have hereunto put my *Seale* (struck through) *hand* (interlined) the Daie & Yeare first above Written.

Witnes to the publishing hereof (signed) Fra: Collyns
Juliyus Shawe
John Robinson
Hamnet Sadler
Robert Whattcott

By me William Shakspeare (signed)

Probatum coram Mag|ist|ro Willi|a|mo Byrde legum d|o|c|t|ore Commissar|io| etc. xxii^do die mensis Junii Anno d|omi|ni 1616 Juram|en|to Johannis Hall unius ex|ecutorum| etc. Cui etc. de bene etc. Jurat|i| Res|er|vata p|o|t|est|ate etc. Sussanne Hall alt|eri| ex|ecutorum| etc. cum ven|er|it etc. petitur

In|ventariu|m ex|hibi|t|um|

On dorse of page three at top: Juratus vir reservetur potestas alii ex|ecu|tricii cum venerit 22 Junii W. Byrde (signed)

right hand: Mr. Shackspere his will
left hand: Mr Shackspere June 16

Six 'authenticated' Shakespeare signatures survive and three of these are on his will. There is one on the Court of Requests document (document 11) in the Public Record Office and the two others are on deeds connected with the purchase of the Blackfriars house, in the British Library and the Guildhall Library respectively. All are reproduced below, with the exception of the first will signature which is of very poor quality.

It is obvious at a glance that these signatures, with the exception of the last two, are not the signatures of the same man. Almost every letter is formed in a different way in each. Literate men in the sixteenth and seventeenth centuries developed personalized signatures much as people do today and it is unthinkable that Shakespeare did not. Which of the signatures reproduced here is the genuine article is anybody's guess. Some scholars, perhaps more familiar with literature than the calligraphy of the period have failed to recognize the problem; Tannenbaum saw a 'striking similarity' between the last will signature and that on the Guildhall deed.[1] The anti-Stratfordians, on the other hand, have argued that Shakespeare did not

[1]S.A. Tannenbaum, *Shakespeare's Penmanship* (New York, 1927) 19.

25a. Signature of Shakespeare on deposition given to the Court of Requests, 1612. Public Record Office (REQ 4/1).

25b. Signature of Shakespeare on vendor's copy of deed of purchase for Blackfriars property, 1613. Reproduced by permission of the Guildhall Library.

25c. Signature of Shakespeare on mortgage deed for Blackfriars property, 11 March 1613. Reproduced by permission of the British Library (Egerton MS 1787).

25d. Signature of Shakespeare on the second page of his will, 1616. Public Record Office (PROB 1/4).

25e. Signature of Shakespeare on the last page of his will, 1616. Public Record Office (PROB 1/4).

25a

25b

25c

25d

25e

sign the documents himself because he was illiterate or that he did sign them, but because he was not used to writing, each time the signature and the spelling was different. An article by Sir Hilary Jenkinson, published in 1922, gives a clue to what the solution might be. It was his opinion that clerks taking down the evidence of witnesses in law suits often 'signed' it with the deponent's name themselves, using a different hand from that which they had used for the body of the text to give it 'an air of verisimilitude'.[1] So much for the signature on the deposition given by Shakespeare to the Court of Requests. If this was the practice in the equity courts, why should it not also have been the practice of attorneys' clerks when drawing up conveyancing documents? Possibly Shakespeare was not even in London to sign the mortgage deed and the deed of purchase for the Blackfriars gatehouse.

The will signatures have been regarded as sacrosanct, in the main, but in the light of Sir Hilary Jenkinson's observations and practice in the Prerogative Court of Canterbury, the authenticity of even these signatures must be questioned. There is a possibility that the so called original will is a facsimile copy made either by the court or by Collins' clerk. The court's ancient practice had been to return the original will to the executor and to keep a copy; among the bundles of wills proved in 1538, for instance, there are hardly any originals. By the time Shakespeare died the court was more likely to keep the original but there are instances of facsimile copies being made for the court's files. The will of John Borlas, part of which is reproduced below, is an example. Borlas's name and the name of the witnesses are in a different hand from each other and from the text of the will and it is only when the paper is turned over that the will is revealed to be *vera copia*. It is not very likely that Shakespeare's will comes into this category as the contemporary copy now kept by the Birthplace Trust is probably the executors' copy which was retained by them when the grant of probate was made and the original was kept by the court. Another possibility is that the clerk who wrote the will 'forged' Shakespeare's signatures. Until the Statute of Frauds of 1667 there was no necessity for a will to bear the testator's signature at all. Manuals of the period indicate the form preferred by the doctors of civil law, namely that a will should be signed on every page and witnessed, but virtually any form was acceptable so long as it seemed to be a true representation of the dying man's wishes. The will of one Jacob Westcombe, proved in 1593, was signed and sealed only by the overseer.[2] Among fifty-five wills proved in the Prerogative Court in the same month as Shakespeare's, there are numerous examples of 'forgeries' of witnesses' signatures;[3] the attorney's clerk simply wrote the names on the document, sometimes using a contrived hand to make them look like signatures, sometimes not. It is not unlikely that Collins' clerk wrote the names of Shaw, Robinson and Sadler on Shakespeare's will; the hands of the three witnesses are suspiciously similar. There is no positive evidence that Shakespeare did not sign his will; the shaky pen strokes certainly look like those made by a sick man. But if one must select one of the four signed documents as being the sole example of our greatest playwright's hand, the will has no better claim than the Requests deposition, the mortgage deed or the Guildhall conveyance. As we have seen, the legal sanctity of the signature was not firmly established; the medieval tradition was that of an illiterate landowning class with scribes to do their writing and signing. Wills were proved by the executor's oath, nothing more, unless objections were raised by some interested party, in which case witnesses would be examined. It was not until later in the seventeenth century that handwriting experts began to be used by the court.

[1] 'Elizabethan Handwriting', *The Library,* 4th series, vol. III, no.I June 1922, 31.

[2] PROB 10/44, May 1593.

[3] PROB 10/332.

26. Will of John Borlas, proved May 1593 in the Prerogative Court of Canterbury. PROB 10/144.

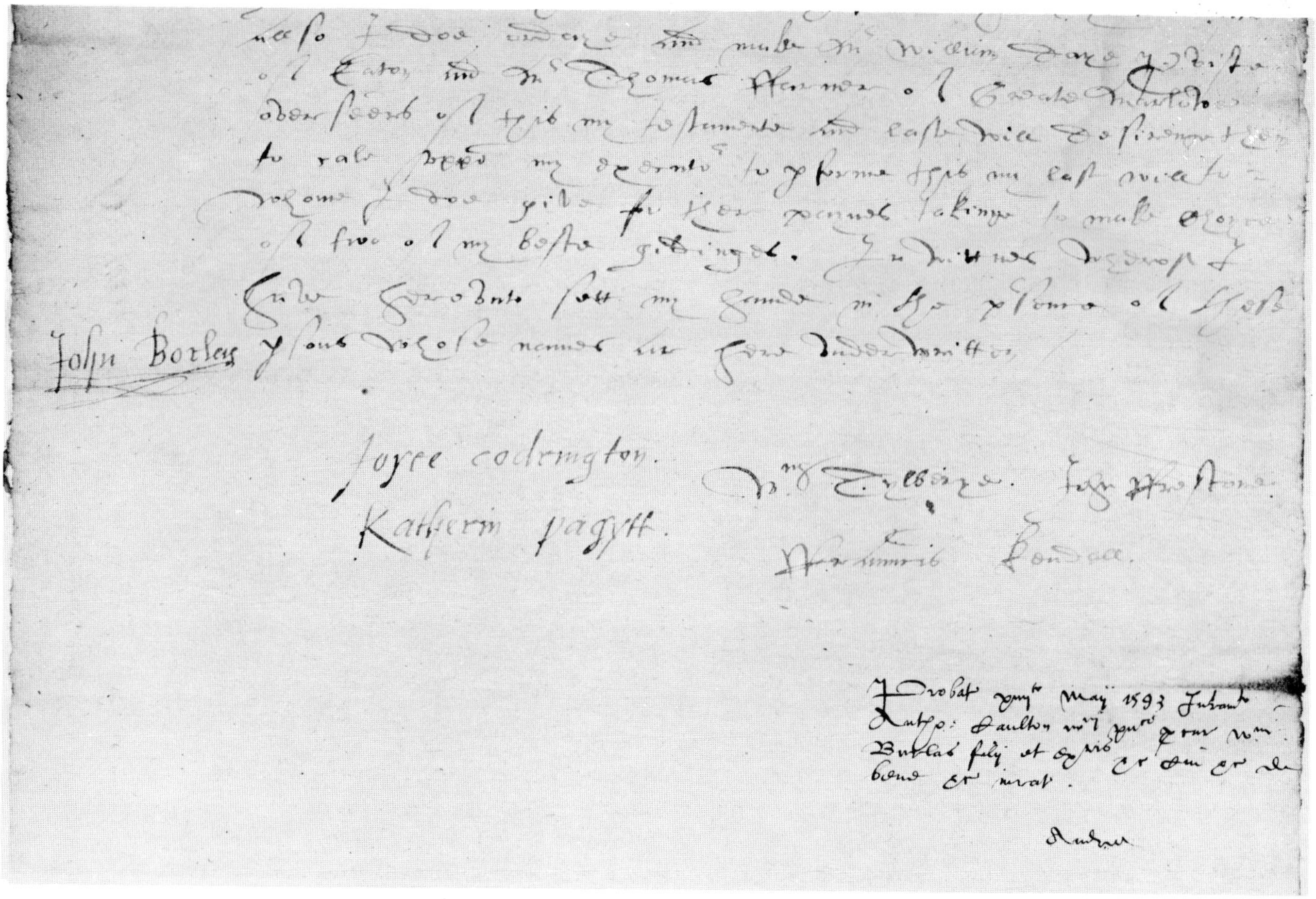
John Borlas

Joyce codrington.

Katherin pagytt.

Documents relating to Shakespeare and his family in the Public Record Office

View of frankpledge taken at Stratford-upon-Avon, 29 April 1552; John Shakespeare and others fined for making a refuse heap in Henley Street (SC 2/207/82). Document 1.

Two conveyances of property in Warwickshire by William Clopton showing John Shakespeare as tenant of Ingon Meadow in the parish of Hampton Lucy, 1570 (C 54/843 mm.10-15). This document was drawn to my attention by Dr Katherine Wyndham.

Exchequer, informations and proceedings against John Shakespeare for usury, 1570 (E 159/359, Recorda, Hil., mm.215,237). The latter document was drawn to my attention by Wendy Goldsmith. Document 3.

Exchequer, record of fine paid by John Shakespeare for usury, 1570 (E159/360, Fines, manucaptiones etc.).

Exchequer, informations against John Shakespeare for illegal purchases of wool, 1572 (E 159/362, Recorda, Hil., m.68d; 363, Recorda, Mich., m.183d.).

Court of Common Pleas, Plea Roll; action by John Shakespeare against John Luther for a debt, 1572 (CP40/1304, m.910d.).

Court of Common Pleas, Plea Roll; action by Henry Higford against John Shakespeare and John Musshen for debt, 1573 and 1578 (CP 40/1313 m.399; 1355 m.7d; 1356 m.1123d.).

Foot of Fine recording the conveyance of two messuages, two gardens and two orchards in Stratford-upon-Avon by Edmund Hall to John Shakespeare, 1575 (CP 25(2)/234 pt.2, Mich., 17 and 18 Eliz I).

Foot of Fine recording a conveyance of property in Wilmcote between John and Mary Shakespeare, George Gibbs, Thomas Webbe and Humphrey Hooper, 1579 (CP 25(2)/235, Hil., 21 Eliz I).

Foot of Fine recording the conveyance of property in Aston Cantlow by John and Mary Shakespeare to Edmund Lambert, 1579 (CP 25(2)/235, East., 21 Eliz I).

Foot of Fine recording the conveyance of property in Snitterfield by John and Mary Shakespeare to Robert Webbe, 1580 (CP 25(2)/235, East., 22 Eliz I).

Exchequer, account of fines imposed in the court of King's Bench: John Shakespeare fined for non-appearance and for failing to bring John Audeley of Nottingham, for whom he had stood surety, into court, 1580 (E 101/109/13, mm.20d-21).

Will of Richard Hathaway (father of William Shakespeare's wife), made 1 September 1581, proved July 1582 (PROB 11/64, s.31).

Exchequer, survey of the manor of Stratford, showing John Shakespeare holding two properties in Henley Street, 1590 (E 178/2351). Document 2.

Certificate by the commissioners for Warwickshire showing John Shakespeare failing to attend church 'for feare of processe for debtte', 25 Sept 1592 (SP 12/243/76). Document 5.

Account of payments by the Treasurer of the Chamber to William Kempe, William Shakespeare and Richard Burbage for performing plays, 1595 (E 351/542, m.207d.). Document 12.

Court of King's Bench, writ of attachment against William Shakespeare, 1596 (KB 29/234). Document 7.

Certificate of the London tax commissioners showing William Shakespeare as a defaulter, 15 November 1597 (E 179/146/354). Document 8.

Indenture by the London tax commissioners listing William Shakespeare as a defaulter, 1 October 1598 (E 179/146/369). Document 9.

Enrolled subsidy account showing Shakespeare as a defaulter for subsidies granted in 1593 and 1597 (E 359/56).

Exchequer, Pipe Roll, entry relating to Shakespeare's debts for the subsidy, 1598-1599 (E 372/444, m.'Residuum London').

Exchequer, Pipe Roll, entry relating to Shakespeare's debt for the subsidy, 1599-1600 (E 372/445, m.'Residuum Sussex'). Document 10.

Court of King's Bench, Coram Rege Roll, complaint of John Shakespeare against John Lambert, relating to property in Wilmcote, 1589 (KB 27/1311, rot. 516). Document 6.

Court of Chancery, case of John and Mary Shakespeare against John Lambert, 1597-1599 (C 2/Eliz/5/24/21; C 33/95 f.140v.; C 33/98 f.57v.).

Concord and Foot of Fine recording Shakespeare's purchase of New Place from William Underhill, 1597 (CP 24(1)/15; CP 25(2)/237, East., 39 Eliz I). Document 21.

Foot of fine by which Hercules Underhill conveyed New Place to William Shakespeare, 1602 (CP25(2)/237, Mich., 44 & 45 Eliz I no. 15).

Court of Common Pleas, Plea Roll; action by John Shakespeare against John Walford for a debt of £21, Trinity Term 1599 (CP 40/1626 rot. 353d.).

Chancery, Inquisition Post Mortem of Thomas Brend, showing Shakespeare and others occupying the Globe playhouse, 16 May 1599 (C 142/257/68).

Examination of Augustine Phillips concerning the performance of *Richard II* before Essex's rebellion, 18 February 1601 (SP 12/278/85). Document 13.

Warrants under the signet and privy seals for the issue of letters patent authorizing Shakespeare and his companions to perform plays throughout the realm under royal patronage, 17 and 18 May 1603 (PSO 2/22; C 82/1690).

Enrolment of letters patent issued under the above-mentioned warrants, 19 May 1603 (C 66/1608, m.4). Document 14.

Account of the Master of the Great Wardrobe recording the issue of red cloth to Shakespeare and his fellows for the entry of King James I into London, 15 March 1604 (LC 2/4(5) f.78). Document 15.

Account of payment to the King's Men for attendance on the Spanish ambassador, 9-27 August 1604 (AO 1/388/41). Document 16.

Will of Augustine Phillips, made 4 May 1605, proved 13 May 1605 (PROB 11/105, s.31). Document 17.

Account of Edmund Tylney, Master of the Revels for 1604-5, listing plays performed (AO 3/908/13). Document 18.

Account of Sir George Buc, Master of the Revels for 1611-12, listing plays performed (AO 3/908/14). Document 19.

Survey of the manor of Rowington, showing Shakespeare holding a cottage in Stratford, 24 October 1604 (E 178/4661). Document 22.

Survey of the manor of Rowington, showing Shakespeare holding a dwelling house in Stratford, 1606 (LR 2/228, f.199r.).

Concord and Foot of Fine recording the confirmation to Shakespeare by William and John Combe of a freehold in Old Stratford, 1610 (CP 24(2)/7; CP 25(2)/365, Trin., 8 James I, no.15).

Court of Requests, case of Stephen Belott against Christopher Mountjoy, 1612 (REQ 4/1; REQ 1/183, f.269r.). Document 11.

Enrolment of a bargain and sale conveying a property in Blackfriars from Henry Walker to Shakespeare, 10 March 1613 (C 54/2184, no.45).

Court of Chancery, Sir Thomas Bendish, William Shakespeare and five others against Matthew Bacon relating to the title to property in Blackfriars, 1615 (C 2/Jas I/Bll; C 33/127, f.1074r.).

Will of John Combe, proved 10 November 1615 (PROB 11/126 s.118). Document 23.

Court of King's Bench, Coram Rege Roll, plea of Thomasine Ostler against her father John Heminges, 1615 (KB 27/1454, rot.692).

Will of William Shakespeare, made 25 March 1616, proved 22 June 1616; registered copy and entry of probate (PROB 1/4; PROB 11/127 s.59; PROB 8/16 f.155r.). Document 24.

Estreat of court roll of Rowington manor showing the admission of Susanna Hall and her husband John to a cottage in Stratford after the death of Shakespeare, 1617 (LR 11/50, no.720).

Court of Requests, case of John Witter against John Heminges and Henry Condell, 1619-20 (REQ 4/1, REQ 1/30, f.761).

Petition of Robert Benfield, Heliard Swanston and Thomas Pollard to the Lord Chamberlain with the answers of Cuthbert, William and Winifred Burbage and John Shanks, 1635 (LC 5/133 pp.44-51). Document 20.

Will of John Hall, Shakespeare's son-in-law, made 25 November 1635, proved 29 November 1636 (PROB 11/172, s.115).

Warrants from the Lord Chamberlain of the Household enclosing a schedule of plays acted at court in the year 1636-7 (AO 3/908/21-3).

Court of Chancery, case of Baldwin Brookes against Susanna Hall and Thomas and Elizabeth Nash, 1637 (C 7/49/115; C 7/180/173).

Documents of doubtful validity

Petition from the players at the Blackfriars to the Privy Council (SP 12/260/117). A petition by Shakespeare, Pope, Burbage, Phillips, Sly and others requesting that the Blackfriars theatre be allowed to remain open. It is widely believed to be a forgery.

Court of King's Bench, Coram Rege Roll, plea of William Shakespeare against John Clayton of Bedfordshire for a debt of £7 in 1600 (KB 27/1361 rot. 293). The plaintiff is not thought to be the dramatist.

Certificate of musters for Warwickshire, 1605 (SP 12/61 f.69v.). A William Shakespeare appears in the list of soldiers of the town of Rowington, but this is almost certainly not the dramatist.

Selective Bibliography

N.E. Evans, *Shakespeare in the Public Records* (Public Record Office Handbooks, no. 5, London, 1964).

S. Schoenbaum, *William Shakespeare: A Documentary Life* (Oxford, 1975).

S. Schoenbaum, *William Shakespeare, Records and Images* (London, 1981).

B. Roland Lewis, *The Shakespeare Documents* (2 vols, Stanford and London, 1940 and 1941).

Leslie Hotson, *Shakespeare versus Shallow* (London, 1931).

Ernest Law, *Some Supposed Shakespeare Forgeries* (London, 1911).

A.E. Stamp, *The Disputed Revels Accounts* (Oxford, 1930).

Mark Eccles, *Shakespeare in Warwickshire* (Madison, 1961).